I am the storm

Jackalyn Storm

BookLeaf
Publishing

Presentation by *BookLeaf Publishing*

Web: www.bookleafpub.com

E-mail: info@bookleafpub.com

ISBN: 9789357696302

First edition 2023

DEDICATION

To my isle, Maria.

I'd spend the rest of my life with you if they'd
let me.

ACKNOWLEDGEMENT

First and foremost Matt. Secondly to my personal leadership team, those who allowed me to feel what I needed to feel whilst laying a road of support and guidance instead of judgement: Pete, Alena, Chris, T-A, Darren & Monka.

A thousand currawongs

The sounds of Darlington's warbles,
The way the convict brick paths wobble.
I make my way to the ruins of Mr Waddle,
The fading of my nightmares - woeful.
Away from this isle I feel stuck, I wallow,
But here I find peace underneath these wattles.

Sounds of the Isle

My footsteps echoed as if I was walking through a large
empty gallery. The only other sounds were provided by
the island herself.
A deep rumble of wind combined with a high pitch
shrill that twisted its sound in circles.
I was almost alone here with only my thoughts and the
island that haunts me through love, for company.

I stepped out of the large convict ruin and into a vortex
of external peace. Without the cracks in the brickwork,
the sounds were silenced.
I, internally tormented, started walking uphill into a
blissful atmosphere.

I walked towards the mob of kangaroos, unafraid.
They watched me,
They predicted my movements and decided they need
not move themselves,
Only the giant male stared me down until I was out of
sight.
I made my path on what precious little grass was
remaining.

I continued walking uphill until I was stopped by a
rubble of bricks,

A fence post,
A sheet of tin,
And an unknown piece of rusted metal undiscovered by
my eyes.

I sat down amongst the ruins surrounded completely by
lomandra and eucalypt.
I absorbed all the new sounds.
Here I was far from alone.
All tiny sounds now.
A hum of cars and civilisation from the mainland,
Buzzing of flies,
The crunches of gum leaves under a wallabies foot.
The calls of wattlebirds,
Waubles of magpies,
And a choir of penguins.
As the colours changed in the sunset,
The temperature dropped and an eerie wind shot its way
through some nearby sheoaks.

I was home,
This is my home. I don't ever want to leave this place.

Morning tea

I was looking for old things,
Man-made island relics.
I headed steeply uphill in an old woodland area.
The weather was perfect for walking,
Low 20s with a slight breeze.
The tourists were overturning the main tracks,
So I had no qualms about going off track to find some inner
peace.

We had rain last night which disturbed my heat-ridden slumber
several times,
Its deafening pelts on the roof.
The dampness combined with the morning hot sun made the
land smell like one big billy of bush tea.
Eucalypt and tea tree aromas filled the air,
The fizz from the earth could be heard amongst the insects and
the squeak of baby currawongs.

My senses were heightened,
Happy and alive.
My heart rate was slow and relaxed despite the sweat I could
feel forming as I continued walking uphill.

I'd been gifted the ability to walk through the bush with
silence.
I walked past jack jumpers that were not irritated by my
presence.

After an hour of reading and listening to the bush I found a
sawn-off stump. Other than this there was no evidence of
humans being here before.
I paused in the shade.
I had forgotten my hat which was foolish.
My body burns black like my ancestors.
But my face burns and peels like my white forefathers.
And if you stop for too long in the bush the flies will find you.
I pick up a broken branch of black gum,
Its leaves dying and faded to a minty yellow.
 I made a thick swoosh sound with the branch as the air got
caught amongst the leaves and the flies left me alone.

Then,
There it was.
The distant sound of wood cutting.
Not with a chainsaw but with the meticulous beat of an axe.
Ghosts.
Souls more so.
Forever stuck with the spirit of Maria and I knew one day I
would join them.

Insomnia

It was 2.50 am and the Island was keeping me awake.
It wasn't the cries of the geese,
Nor the hens scaring off a wild devil.
It wasn't the thump of the wallabies' tails on the hillside above,
Nor the screech of a rare possum.
It wasn't the rain pelting on the roof,
Nor the waves crashing on the beach below.
And it wasn't the howl of the wind that ripped through the whole island reminding you who really owned the place.
It wasn't these things as I was 160 km away.
It was precisely these things not keeping me awake, that was keeping me awake.
I was not just heartbroken but I was broken in spirit too.
I found no purpose to live for,
I tried to find beauty and joy but the world was very black and white.
As black and white as the bureaucracy that discarded me.

The way time heals

Tick,
Tock.
Tick,
Tock.
Tick,
Tock.

How bizarre that the sound of the clock
constantly exists,
How does it go unnoticed for so long while the
sound still emits?

The clock still ticking,
The clock still tocking.
But it's not heard.
Until, a moment later the ticks become loud,
and the tocks even louder still.

They compete to be the largest sound in a quiet
room against only our breaths.
My breaths.
One breath in for a tick tock.
One breath out for the next tick tock.

There was a third sound in my darkened
bedroom that now appeared,
Me.
The voice inside my head that automated my
movements.
The voice that says put the bread in the toaster,
And take the butter from the fridge. The same
voice that now mimics the insults of my former
managers.

Three sounds do their thing as if in a symphony.
The clock clicks as it tells time.
The air as it moves in and out of my lungs,
Now faster.
One breath in for every tick,
One breath out for every tock.
And my internal voice chanting words of every
possible reason for why I was sacked.

The insults repeat and jar in bullet points.
Because of this,
Because of that.
This,
That,
This,
That.

Tick tock.
Tick tock.
Tick tock.

And then a moment later,
The sounds quieten.
My senses switched,
I was now entirely focused on pain.

My teeth from grinding
My jaw from clenching.
My knees from spending far too long curled up.

Finally a tear fell,
and I was asleep.

Souls together - bodies apart.

Every night before I sleep I let out this sobbing wail,
A howl at the gods for allowing such a hell to
approach my earth.
The only thing that stops the deep stabbing pain is to
close my eyes and take a walk around my Isle,
My heart rate drops,
My jaw relaxes and the pulsating throb subsides.
I visualise every stick,
Every crumble of brick,
Every shade of gum leaf.
I can isolate the individual calls of birds.
I see life near, and I see life far.
I take the extensions which are my feet and I start
walking.
I can feel it in my mind because my soul is there,
Forever amongst the farmland and trees with all the
others who lived and loved fiercely.
My body now an empty, sad and broken shell tries
desperately to reunite and return back home.

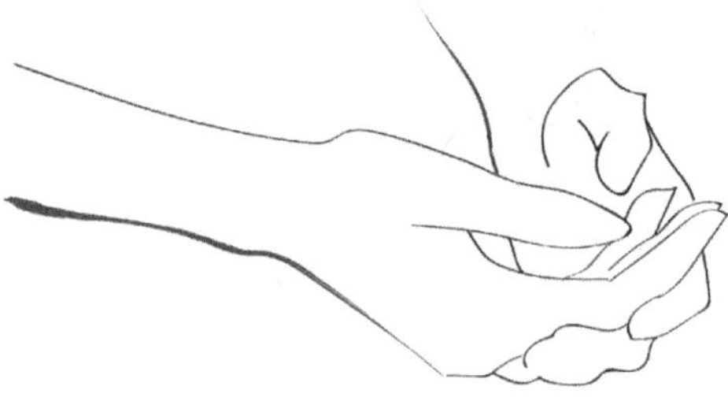

Far away from home.

Shuffle left,
Shuffle right,
Shuffle left again.

I had no desire to exert myself more than this
slow form of walking.
I made my way around the abandoned
showgrounds,
Hidden in the dark.

There was no one else here,
The community was tucked up in bed.
They were in their homes,
Feeling warm,
Feeling loved.

Shuffle right,
Shuffle left,
Shuffle right again.

The warning cries of some Masked Lapwings
filled the night.
They did not want me here,
I tried to shuffle faster.

My features felt so heavy and flat against my
face,
I had no energy spare to control them.
They sat there in solidarity being sad.

My skin was heavy and spotty,
My eyes were heavy without spark,
My cheeks heavy and bloated,
My lips heavy and downturned,
My hair heavy and greasy,
Even the weight of my ears felt sad.
I was a sorry sight indeed.

As I made my way around the circular oval, I
heard the sound of frogs,
A lone car drove past heading to their home.
I neared the road and fell to my knees.
I cried.
How could they do this to me?

Goodnight ghosts

I felt the smooth texture of the heavy-duty paint
on the large double door,
And I push it into its place for the night.
My right hand grabs the weight of the latch,
I feel it weigh my palm down,
I twist the weight around and settle it into its
lock,
And I hear the sound of the metal hitting itself.
I turn around and feel the dust beneath my feet
slowly degrading from the 200-year-old bricks.
I walk across the bricks,
Just seven steps to switch off the lights,
My final duty for the night.
I walk faster towards the last opened door,
Here I play with the island as it fights me to
close,
I laugh,
Please let me go home,
My muscles flexed,
I grunt with the wind,
I heave the door into place.
I slide the bolt across and attach the padlock.
My thumb is on the base,
And fingertips feel the curve of the lock.

Just four steps and I am on the grass,
I make my way down the slight slope to the
road.
I see each blade of grass and pray for it to grow.
A large leap off the concrete,
Now my feet glide gracefully up the road,
My legs feel short and a part of this earth.
I see the ducks,
I see the reflection in the creek,
I hear some hens,
I see the clouds,
The shades of blue and yellow and green and
grey.
I taste this,
I smell this,
I hear this,
I feel this,
I try so hard to grab all this from my memory.
I try to pull it out of my skull so I can live it one
more time.
Oh! What I would give just to touch the door of
the old Commissariat Store and close that
building one last time.
I try desperately again to materialise my
memory into reality.
Please, please, please take me back.
My eyelids tighten,
My lips pursed as if compressing my face may
put me back on that convict isle.

With hopelessness I cry,
My chest in painful sharp compressions moves
with my sobs.
It hurts so much.

Southerly prayer

My feet went up,
Then my feet went down.
They left deep impressions in the sand,
There was no magnetic extension here.
No connection to place,
nor songs on the cutting wind.

With the foreign waves as a backdrop,
I sang a prayer up to the heavens.

Take me back to the south land,
Take me back to my songs.
Take me back to the mountains that love me,
A sky that holds me and to the oceans I call my own.
Take me home.

I'm not welcome here

All the salt was evaporating even the oxygen
from the air,
And I was suffocating slowly.
Trapped in myself as I died of depression,
monotony and boredom.
The people around me seem so starved of
creativity and life that I felt so alone as I
observed the circus going on around me.
It wasn't a circus full of life or wonders,
It was a freakshow full of beige and small
minds.

They drank to talk to each other,
I drank to numb the voices in my head.
Even though it was the only decent conversation
I had had all day.

Rock bottom is this way

Imagine a really big funnel,
For the sake of our imagination let's make the
funnel beige.
The big beige funnel made of plastic has also
faded like mothers' tupperware,
This funnel represents my new town.

Imagine a glass marble,
Now that's me.
I get dropped in the funnel,
I start rotating around the plastic.
First making quite a large circumnavigation of
the large piece in our imagination,
But as gravity takes effect my circular rotations
get smaller and smaller,
But also faster and faster.
Very soon I'm going to fall through the spout
and into a bucket of unknown,
It's this pail that scares me.

I had lived previously in harmonic solitude,
With tranquility and peace and a balanced mind
on multitudes of wavelengths.
This town while isolated,
Was not calm but crazy.

I spiraled around the town,
I absorbed all that it was emitting,
And I started losing marbles.

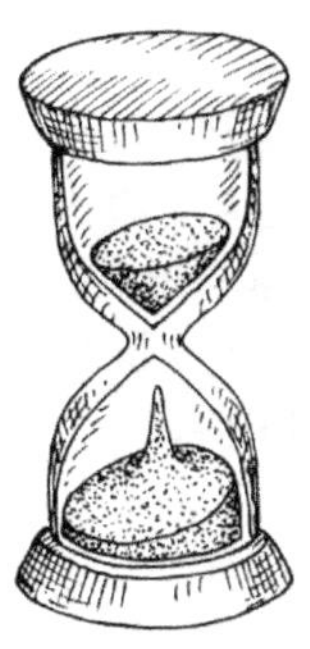

Back on my map

I looked out across the seas,
And I saw my island waiting for me.

How the waves of the passage rocked and
soothed me,
Because I felt as small as a crying baby,
And they hushed me with comfort.

When I stepped off the ship,
It was like I could see from one side of the
island to the other.
There was so much depth in my vision.
I wasn't just looking at bracken and blackwoods,
I was seeing every single frond,
Every individual yellow ball of wattle,
All with sharpened intense detail.
Was I dreaming?

In my sleep for the past year I had traced this
map.
I traced its coastline,
Its coves,
Its points,
and its bays.
Now at last I could trace all this with my feet.
I could touch my dreams.

I was away for 470 days.
And while I was back for just one day,
I had topped up the colour of my memory
palette.

Home for Christmas

My soul was waiting for me in the old
campground,
And she filled me right up.
Even the freckles on my face could feel.
I extended my feet from their earthly
connections and admired the orbital grandeur of
the gullys blackwoods.
I stopped.
As one we heard the sounds of those with wings,
We heard insects,
We heard thornbills,
We heard rosellas.

I continued my journey reunited with life.
We covered as much land as we could.
We were rugged up in a big, natural soft blanket.
We sat in the corner of Howell's cottage,
We laid in the circle of The Mill,
We kneeled on Charle's grave,
Familiarity.
I was home.
In every nook and cranny the island comforted
me,
With a big, safe, warm hug.
Albeit temporary,
I cuddled my soul until I was forced to go.

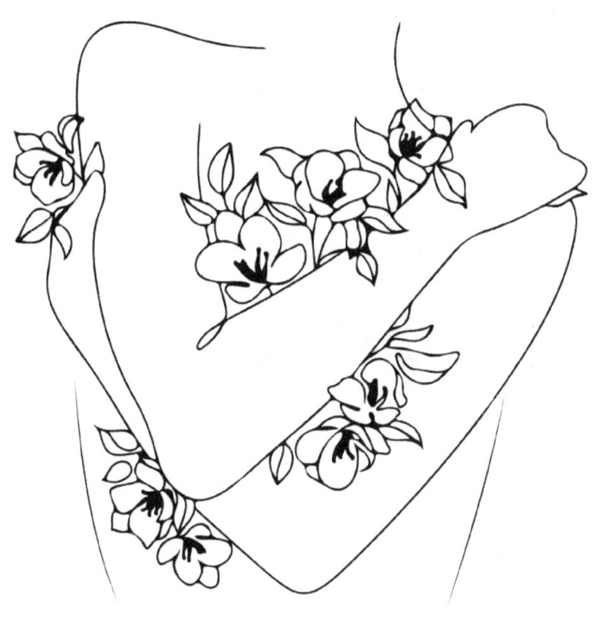

Put your boots on and head south

Mercury Passage had become to me a scene in Fair
Verona.
A Shakespearean separation,
A rotation of grief,
That I kept failing to complete,
Instead becoming an internal vortex of love, sadness
and loneliness.

What was a game of internal politics on one side,
Was a battle of survival for my side.

After years of torment and sleepless nights,
I realised the only way to move forward was to return
to my mother.

You need to make your heart sing again, a friend had
said to me.
An epiphany,
As I had assumed my heart was incapable of melody
or tune, without my beloved isle.

My heart sang before Maria,
On the mountain where I was raised.
The mountain my human mother had carried me
across.

The tracks I explored alone to find solace as a
teenager,
and the same landscape I hope will bring me peace as
I rediscover them in my middle age.

I put my boots on and I started walking south.

O'Gradys Falls - midwinter

I hadn't needed to bring my canvas pack for the
short 2 km return walk,
But I had wanted to feel like a child on an
adventure -
To reset myself,
And my accustomed way of thinking.

I breathed in and breathed out,
Releasing negativity.
I saw one lone bird,
The currawong.

I looked up and saw the organ pipes so close,
I felt as if I could reach and touch them.
They played hide and seek between a band of
thin cloud.

My senses still now.
All I could hear was the horse-like sound of the
falls which lay ahead.
In recent years I had followed roads all over
Tasmania,
Chasing grand tourist scenes.
These falls were nothing like St Columba or
Montezuma,

But,
To scale,
I felt like a safe child in their presence.
No hoard of tourists with cameras,
Just myself,
Mother Mountain,
My memories,
And one currawong whom I was sure was
watching me.

She is wild

Soon this water will pass by our Ranelagh
window before flowing further towards the sea,
Where some people will drive over the concrete
bridge at Huonville never knowing how wild
that water would be.

The wader

Living amongst the bay,
And the beach that crescents the turquoise waves,
Lives an oystercatcher,
Who is staring out to the azure sea.

His calls echo against the nearby cliffs,
Peep, peep, peep.
A sad lonely sound coming from his bright red
beak.

Through winter he battles Earth's elements
everyday,
With cold winter winds that are funneled through
the bay.
In spring he battles the high tidal waves,
That threatened to take his nest away.

By the time summer has come,
The weather has calmed,
And the days are long.
Nine months he has spent all alone,
Until now, as the humans have come from their
homes.

The sound of people is the sound of destruction.
They bring with them all of nature's irritations,
In the form of dogs and bikes, music and
campfires,
Threatening the locals just trying to survive.
Their four-wheel drives crush their nests,
While children playing games break their eggs.

The oystercatchers warning is heard all summer
long,
Peep, peep, peep.
Until the humans have all gone.

Sense at last

I hear birds sing these days,
If I'm paddling on the freshwater river,
Or walking along lonely coastal shores,
Or climbing mountains of great heights,
I hear them.

I smell the aroma of flowers these days,
If I'm sitting in a tea garden,
Or discovering old tracks lost amongst native
shrubs,
Or shopping at a market with a bouquet store,
I smell them.

I see joy these days,
If I'm attending a party for my friends' children,
Or watching a comedy at the theater,
Or making jokes with colleagues at morning tea,
I see fun.

I taste sweet things these days,
If I'm drinking cocktails with friends,
Or picking blackberries along the garden fence,
Or toasting marshmallows at a nighttime event.
I taste sweetness.

I touch love these days,
If I'm holding my dearest in an embrace,
Or patting my cats on a cold winter's day,
While we rug up in a blanket my mother made,
I touch love.

And while I hear, smell, see, taste and touch
happiness these days,
There will always be a slight sadness within my
gaze.
For my soul remains forever with Maria's Isle,
But when I dream of her every night, I now do
so with a smile.